foundations

SMALL GROUP STUDY

taught by tom holladay and kay warren

G O D

ZONDERVAN®   SADDLEBACK CHURCH

ZONDERVAN.com/
AUTHORTRACKER
follow your favorite authors

ZONDERVAN®

Foundations: *God Study Guide*
Copyright © 2003, 2008 by Tom Holladay and Kay Warren

Requests for information should be addressed to:
Zondervan, *Grand Rapids, Michigan* 49530

ISBN 978-0-310-27672-2

08 09 10 11 12 13 14 15 16 17 18 • 23 22 21 20 19 18 17 16 15 14 13 12 11 10 9 8 7 6 5 4 3 2 1

FOREWORD

What *Foundations* Will Do for You

I once built a log cabin in the Sierra mountains of northern California. After ten backbreaking weeks of clearing forest land, all I had to show for my effort was a leveled and squared concrete foundation. I was discouraged, but my father, who built over a hundred church buildings in his lifetime, said, "Cheer up, son! Once you've laid the foundation, the most important work is behind you." I've since learned that this is a principle for all of life: you can never build *anything* larger than the foundation can handle.

The foundation of any building determines both its size and strength, and the same is true of our lives. A life built on a false or faulty foundation will never reach the height that God intends for it to reach. If you skimp on your foundation, you limit your life.

That's why this material is so vitally important. *Foundations* is the biblical basis of a purpose-driven life. You must understand these life-changing truths to enjoy God's purposes for you. This curriculum has been taught, tested, and refined over ten years with thousands of people at Saddleback Church. I've often said that *Foundations* is the most important class in our church.

Why You Need a Biblical Foundation for Life

- *It's the source of personal growth and stability.* So many of the problems in our lives are caused by faulty thinking. That's why Jesus said the truth will set us free and why Colossians 2:7a (CEV) says, *"Plant your roots in Christ and let him be the foundation for your life."*

- *It's the underpinning of a healthy family.* Proverbs 24:3 (TEV) says, *"Homes are built on the foundation of wisdom and understanding."* In a world that is constantly changing, strong families are based on God's unchanging truth.

- *It's the starting point of leadership.* You can never lead people farther than you've gone yourself. Proverbs 16:12b (MSG) says, *"Sound leadership has a moral foundation."*

- *It's the basis for your eternal reward in heaven.* Paul said, *"Whatever we build on that foundation will be tested by fire on the day of judgment . . . We will be rewarded if our building is left standing"* (1 Corinthians 3:12, 14 CEV).

- *God's truth is the only foundation that will last.* The Bible tells us that *"the sound, wholesome teachings of the Lord Jesus Christ . . . are the foundation for a godly life"* (1 Timothy 6:3 NLT), and that *"God's truth stands firm like a foundation stone . . . "* (2 Timothy 2:19 NLT).

Jesus concluded his Sermon on the Mount with a story illustrating this important truth. Two houses were built on different foundations. The house built on sand was destroyed when rain, floods, and wind swept it away. But the house built on the foundation of solid rock remained firm. He concluded, *"Therefore everyone who hears these words of mine and puts them into practice is like a wise man who built his house on the rock"* (Matthew 7:24 NIV). *The Message* paraphrase of this verse shows how important this is: *"These words I speak to you are not incidental additions to your life . . . They are foundational words, words to build a life on."*

I cannot recommend this curriculum more highly to you. It has changed our church, our staff, and thousands of lives. For too long, too many have thought of theology as something that doesn't relate to our everyday lives, but *Foundations* explodes that mold. This study makes it clear that the foundation of what we do and say in each day of our lives is what we believe. I am thrilled that this in-depth, life-changing curriculum is now being made available for everyone to use.

— Rick Warren, author of *The Purpose Driven® Life*

PREFACE

Get ready for a radical statement, a pronouncement sure to make you wonder if we've lost our grip on reality: *There is nothing more exciting than doctrine!*

Track with us for a second on this. Doctrine is the study of what God has to say. What God has to say is always the truth. The truth gives me the right perspective on myself and on the world around me. The right perspective results in decisions of faith and experiences of joy. *That is exciting!*

The objective of *Foundations* is to present the basic truths of the Christian faith in a simple, systematic, and life-changing way. In other words, to teach doctrine. The question is, why? In a world in which people's lives are filled with crying needs, why teach doctrine? Because biblical doctrine has the answer to many of those crying needs! Please don't see this as a clash between needs-oriented and doctrine-oriented teaching. The truth is we need both. We all need to learn how to deal with worry in our lives. One of the keys to dealing with worry is an understanding of the biblical doctrine of the hope of heaven. Couples need to know what the Bible says about how to have a better marriage. They also need a deeper understanding of the doctrine of the Fatherhood of God, giving the assurance of God's love upon which all healthy relationships are built. Parents need to understand the Bible's practical insights for raising kids. They also need an understanding of the sovereignty of God, a certainty of the fact that God is in control, that will carry them through the inevitable ups and downs of being a parent. Doctrinal truth meets our deepest needs.

Welcome to a study that will have a lifelong impact on the way that you look at everything around you and above you and within you. Helping you develop a "Christian worldview" is our goal as the writers of this study. A Christian worldview is the ability to see everything through the filter of God's truth. The time you dedicate to this study will lay a foundation for new perspectives that will have tremendous benefits for the rest of your life. This study will help you to:

- Lessen the stress in everyday life

- See the real potential for growth the Lord has given you

- Increase your sense of security in an often troubling world

- Find new tools for helping others (your friends, your family, your children) find the right perspective on life

- Fall more deeply in love with the Lord

Throughout this study you'll see four types of sidebar sections designed to help you connect with the truths God tells us about himself, ourselves, and this world.

- *A Fresh Word:* One aspect of doctrine that makes people nervous is the "big words." Throughout this study we'll take a fresh look at these words, words like *omnipotent* and *sovereign*.

- *A Closer Look:* We'll take time to expand on a truth or look at it from a different perspective.

- *Key Personal Perspective:* The truth of doctrine always has a profound impact on our lives. In this section we'll focus on that personal impact.

- *Living on Purpose:* James 1:22 (NCV) says, *"Do what God's teaching says; when you only listen and do nothing, you are fooling yourselves."* In his book, *The Purpose Driven Life*, Rick Warren identifies God's five purposes for our lives. They are worship, fellowship, discipleship, ministry, and evangelism. We will focus on one or two of these five purposes in each lesson, and discuss how it relates to the subject of the study. This section is very important, so please be sure to leave time for it.

Here is a brief explanation of the other features of this study guide.

Looking Ahead/Catching Up: You will open each meeting with an opportunity for everyone to check in with each other about how you are doing with the weekly assignments. Accountability is a key to success in this study!

Key Verse: Each week you will find a key verse or Scripture passage for your group to read together. If someone in the group has a different translation, ask them to read it aloud so the group can get a bigger picture of the meaning of the passage.

Video Lesson: There is a video lesson segment for the group to watch together each week. Take notes in the lesson outlines as you watch the video, and be sure to refer back to these notes during your discussion time.

Discovery Questions: Each video segment is complemented by questions for group discussion. Please don't feel pressured to discuss every single question. The material in this study is meant to be your servant, not your master, so there is no reason to rush through the answers. Give everyone ample opportunity to share their thoughts. If you don't get through all of the discovery questions, that's okay.

Prayer Direction: At the end of each session you will find suggestions for your group prayer time. Praying together is one of the greatest privileges of small group life. Please don't take it for granted.

Get ready for God to do incredible things in your life as you begin the adventure of learning more deeply about the most exciting message in the world: the truth about God!

— Tom Holladay and Kay Warren

How to Use This Video Curriculum

Here is a brief explanation of the features on your small group DVD. These features include a *Group Lifter* four *Video Teaching Sessions* by Tom Holladay and Kay Warren and a short video, *How to Become a Follower of Christ*, by Rick Warren. Here's how they work:

The *Group Lifter* is a brief video introduction by Tom Holladay giving you a sense of the objective and purpose of this *Foundations* study on God. Watch it together as a group at the beginning of your first session.

The *Video Teaching Sessions* provide you with the teaching for each week of the study. Watch these features with your group. After watching the video teaching session, continue in your study by working through the discussion questions and activities in the study guide.

Nothing is more important than the decision you make to accept Jesus Christ as your Lord and Savior. You will have the option to watch a short video presentation, *How to Become a Follower of Jesus Christ*, at the end of Session One. In this brief video segment, Rick Warren explains the importance of having Christ as the Savior of your life and how you can become part of the family of God. If everyone in your group is already a follower of Christ, or if you feel there is a better time to play this segment, just continue your session by turning to the Discovery Questions in your DVD study guide. You can also select this video presentation separately on the Main Menu of the DVD for viewing at any time.

Follow these simple steps for a successful small group session:

1. Hosts: Watch the video session and write down your answers to the discussion questions in the study guide before your group arrives.

2. Group: Open your group meeting by using the "Looking Ahead" or "Catching Up" section of your lesson.

3. Group: Watch the video teaching lesson and follow along in the outlines in the study guide.

4. Group: Complete the rest of the discussion materials for each session in the study guide.

It's just that simple. Have a great study together!

1

Session One

WHAT IS GOD LIKE?

LOOKING AHEAD

1. What do you hope to get out of this small group study?

2. When you think of God, do you have a picture in your mind? These pictures could be thoughts you've had since childhood, or they might be pictures you've formed more recently as the result of current events, the media, or circumstances in your own life. Share how your picture of God has impacted your life.

Key Verse

The heavens declare the glory of God;
the skies proclaim the work of his hands.

Psalm 19:1 (NIV)

BIBLE TEACHING
Watch the video lesson now and take notes in your outline on pages 3–5.

What comes into our minds when we think about God is the most important thing about us.[1]

— A. W. Tozer

If you can understand it, it's not God.

— Augustine

Children have a way of asking the _____ .

As we look at God's existence, we need to remember three key truths:

1. God is _____ .

2. God is _____ .

3. God is _____ .

God Is Real

God is not a character in a story, in some fairy tale. He is as real as we are.

How do we know God exists?

1. We see God's _____ in what he has made (Genesis 1:1; Romans 1:19–20; Acts 14:16–17).

   > [1]The heavens declare the glory of God; the skies proclaim the work of his hands. [2]Day after day they pour forth speech; night after night they display knowledge. (Psalm 19:1–2 NIV)

---

[1] A. W. Tozer, _Knowledge of the Holy_ (New York: Harper and Row, 1961), 9.

2. We see God's _____ on human history.

> ²⁶*From one man he made every nation of men, that they should inhabit the whole earth; and he determined the times set for them and the exact places where they should live.* ²⁷*God did this so that men would seek him and perhaps reach out for him and find him, though he is not far from each one of us.* (Acts 17:26–27 NIV)

3. We've seen God's _____ in our own lives.

Look at the story of Elijah and his battle with the false prophets on Mount Carmel in 1 Kings 18:24–39.

A CLOSER LOOK

What Does God Look Like?

The Bible tells us that no one has actually seen God (John 1:18). God is spirit (Psalm 139:7–12; John 4:24); God is invisible (John 1:18; Colossians 1:15; Hebrews 11:27). The natural assumption, when hearing the phrase that we are all "made in his image," is to think that God must look something like us—with two arms and two legs. What a scary thought! God, who fills this universe, obviously couldn't look like a man. When the Bible speaks of God having "strong arms" or "sheltering wings," these are not literal descriptions but pictures of how God relates to us.

God Is Revealed

God is not discovered by us, he *reveals himself* to us (Genesis 35:7; Psalm 98:2).

1. God's _____ of himself.

> *From the time the world was created, people have seen the earth and sky and all that God made. They can clearly see his invisible qualities—his eternal power and divine nature. So they have no excuse whatsoever for not knowing God.* (Romans 1:20 NLT)

2. God reveals himself through _____ .

> [20]Above all, you must understand that no prophecy in
> Scripture ever came from the prophets themselves [21]or because
> they wanted to prophesy. It was the Holy Spirit who moved
> the prophets to speak from God. (2 Peter 1:20–21 NLT)

3. God reveals himself through _____ .

> No one has seen God at any time; the only begotten God
> who is in the bosom of the Father, He has explained Him.
> (John 1:18 NASB)

Jesus came to give us understanding (1 John 5:20), and he chose
to reveal the Father to us (Matthew 11:27). God has revealed himself
in many ways, but his last word and clearest revelation is in Jesus
(Hebrew 1:1–2).

Gallup surveys consistently show 96 percent of Americans believe God
is real. For most people, God's existence is not the issue. The real issue
is, "What kind of a God is he?" What does Jesus reveal to us about God?

"HOW TO BECOME A FOLLOWER OF JESUS CHRIST"

Have you ever surrendered your life to Jesus Christ? Take a few minutes with
your group to watch a brief video by Pastor Rick Warren on how to become
part of the family of God. It is included on the menu of this DVD.

DISCOVERY QUESTIONS

1. After going through today's lesson, has your picture of God changed at all? What key truths most influenced the change in your picture?

2. God seems real to people in different ways. Some see him in his creation, some through reading the Bible, some in looking at the history of humanity, and still others through time spent at a church service. What makes God seem the most real to you?

3. God was powerfully present with Elijah in his contest against the prophets of Baal (1 Kings 18:24–39). The same God is present with us today. How have you seen God's actions in your life? Where would you like God to "show up" in your life and work in a powerful way?

4. How does the reality of God affect the decisions you make in your daily life?

5. How do you see the reality of God modeled in your small group?

Did You Get It? How has this week's study helped you see that God is more powerful and real than anything else in your life?

Share with Someone: Think of a person you can encourage with the truth you learned in this session. Write their name in the space below and pray for God to provide that opportunity this week.

LIVING ON PURPOSE

Worship

Following are some ways you can worship God and his reality in your life. Choose one and be prepared to discuss next week how worshiping God in this way changed how you related to yourself, your circumstances, and others.

1. Before the next session, read the following passages of Scripture, in which God speaks about his reality. As you read, focus on listening to God. Hear him speaking directly and personally to you.

   "You are my witnesses," declares the LORD, "and my servant whom I have chosen, so that you may know and believe me and understand that I am he. Before me no god was formed, nor will there be one after me." (Isaiah 43:10 NIV)

   "See now that I myself am He! There is no god besides me. I put to death and I bring to life, I have wounded and I will heal . . . " (Deuteronomy 32:39 NIV)

   6"This is what the LORD says—Israel's King and Redeemer, the LORD Almighty: I am the first and I am the last; apart from me there is no God . . . 8Do not tremble, do not be afraid. Did I not proclaim this and foretell it long ago? You are my witnesses. Is there any God besides me? No, there is no other Rock; I know not one." (Isaiah 44:6, 8 NIV)

2. Concentrate on God's power and control as you remember some of the significant things he has done in your life.

   You don't have to be a history major to see God's work in human history. Think about the fact that all of history is divided by the life of Christ. Consider how history has shown us that the most powerful of human governments rise and fall. Get out a piece of paper and use it to finish the sentence, "God, I see your control over human history when I look at . . . "

   Now finish the sentence, "God, I see your control over my life when I look at . . . "

3. Consider God's beauty and creativity as you close your eyes and think about something he has made. Better yet, get out there and see it! Take a trip to the beach or a beautiful park. Think about what you are seeing and what it says to you about God.

PRAYER DIRECTION

Take some time as a group to pray for one another's specific prayer requests.

NOTES

2

Session two

GOD IS RELATIONAL

Catching Up

1. How did the truth you learned about God in our last session impact your life this week?

2. Were you able to share that truth with someone else?

Key Verse

*How great is the love the Father has
lavished on us, that we should be called children
of God! And that is what we are!
The reason the world does not know us
is that it did not know him.*

1 John 3:1 (NIV)

BIBLE TEACHING
Watch the video lesson now and take notes in your outline on pages 13–16.

God Is Relational

Three Truths about God *(continued)*

1. God is REAL.

2. God is REVEALED.

3. God is _____.

Let's look at some popular ideas about what kind of a God lives in heaven, and see what the Bible has to say about the real God.

The Truth about God

- *The popular idea is:* God is distant.
- *The truth is:* God is _____ (Psalm 139:7–12; James 4:8).

- *The popular idea is:* God watches our actions from afar.
- *The truth is:* God is intimately involved in _____ of our lives (Matthew 6:25–30; Luke 12:6–7).

- *The popular idea is:* God is anxiously waiting to judge those who do wrong.
- *The truth is:* God is waiting to _____ all who ask (John 3:17).

- *The popular idea is:* God is either powerless against or doesn't care much about the evil in the world.

- *The truth is:* God allows an evil world to continue to exist so that more people might be _____ out of it (2 Peter 3:8–9).

A FRESH WORD

Attributes of God

Four theological words provide the background for the statements we've covered about the real person of God.

1. **God's** _____ : God is awesomely near to all of us. God is not beyond the farthest star; he is as near as our next heartbeat. He does not just watch us; he is with us.

2. **God's** _____ : God is everywhere (omni = all + present). His presence fills the universe. He is everyplace all at once.

3. **God's** _____ : God knows everything (omni = all + scient = knowing). He knows everything that has happened, is happening, and will happen. He knows what I will think before I think it.

4. **God's** _____ : God is almighty (omni = all + potent = power). He has the power to do anything he wants. Immediately!

To sum it up:

- In a world in which people see God as _____ , the truth is that God is _____ .

- The number one way we see that God is relational: Jesus taught us to call God our _____ .

God relates to us as a perfect Father.

1. Our Father is willing to make _____ .
   He sent his Son into the world to die as our Savior (John 3:16; 1 John 4:14).

2. Our Father has _____ and _____ for his children (Psalm 103:13; 2 Corinthians 1:3).

3. Our Father _____ his children (Proverbs 3:12).

4. Our Father knows _____ before we ask (Matthew 6:8; 7:9–11); that's why we pray "Our Father" (Matthew 6:9).

5. Our Father _____ us (Matthew 6:20; Hebrews 11:6).

6. Our Father makes us _____ (Romans 8:15–17).

7. Our Father _____ us (2 Thessalonians 2:16–17).

8. Our Father shows no _____ among his children.

   - He gives access to all equally (Ephesians 2:18).

   - He blesses all richly (Romans 10:12).

   - He judges each person impartially (1 Peter 1:17).

Jesus told us: " . . . *Anyone who has seen me has seen the Father . . .* " (John 14:9 NIV)

KEY PERSONAL PERSPECTIVE

God As a Father

You may be having a hard time thinking of God as a Father because of the poor father you had growing up. One of the most refreshing breakthroughs in your life will happen when you begin to see God as the Father you never had, to see God as the Father who fulfills what your father never was.

To strengthen this perspective in your life pray the following prayer. (Pray those parts that are appropriate for your life and add to the prayer where you need to.)

God, I now accept you as the Father I never had. I was disappointed by my earthly father, but you will never disappoint me. I never knew my earthly father, but you want to know me. I was hurt by my earthly father, but I am healed by you. I was ignored by my earthly father, but I have your full and constant attention. I could never meet the expectations of my earthly father, but I can find freedom from expectations in your grace. Amen.

Maybe you had an earthly father who, although he was not perfect, gave you the kind of love that put you on the road to finding a relationship with God through Jesus. You can pray,

Thank you, God, for my earthly father. I know he wasn't perfect in the way he raised me, but he was good and he was kind and he was a man of character. He made decisions in his life that helped me see a little bit of what you are like, decisions that made it easier for me to get to know you. Thank you for the gift he gave me. Amen.

Truth can seem cold and distant until we see how it fits into our lives. How does the truth of God's reality fit you in a personal way? Worship!

Worship is _____ like God is your Father.

Make no mistake, he is your Father if you have put your faith in Christ. The problem is we often don't act like it. We act like God is a distant friend or a terrible tyrant or (heaven help us) a business partner. He is your Father in heaven!

DISCOVERY QUESTIONS

It's okay to admit some truths in the Bible are harder to accept than others. We may know it's all true, but have a difficult time feeling some of God's truths. As you begin this discussion time, be honest about what truths you find easier said than accepted.

1. Look again at the list of popular ideas about God versus the real truths about God. Which popular idea from the list do you think is potentially the most damaging?

2. What is it about God's love that most helps you see him as a perfect Father? How has God shown his love as a Father to you? (From the teaching outline, look again at the list of eight things we know about God as our Father and let them help you think of some personal illustrations of his love.)

One of the healthiest things we can do as believers is to be reminded of the ways in which God has demonstrated his fatherly love toward us, and celebrate the uniqueness of his love. Be aware, though, that many people struggle with the fact that their fathers did not love them the way they needed to be loved. As a result, they struggle with the image of God as their heavenly Father. They are uncertain God can fill the void left by fathers who failed to show them love and support. Help your group see that only the love of God our Father can fill that gigantic hole.

3. Share one aspect of this week's study that was especially meaningful to you.

Did You Get It? How has this week's study helped you see that God is a Father who loves you, no matter what?

Share with Someone: Think of a person you can encourage with the truth you learned in this session. Write their name in the space below and pray for God to provide the opportunity this week.

LIVING ON PURPOSE

Fellowship

The Bible teaches that if you have received Jesus Christ as your Savior, you are now a child of God.

> *Yet to all who received him, to those who believed in his name, he gave the right to become children of God . . .* (John 1:12 NIV)

> 3:26*You are all sons of God through faith in Christ Jesus . . .* 4:6*Because you are sons, God sent the Spirit of his Son into out hearts, the Spirit who calls out, "Abba, Father."* (Galatians 3:26, 4:6 NIV)

If God is your Father, that means everyone else in your small group is your brother or sister in Christ. Talk about what it means to be a part of the family of God. As brothers and sisters in Christ, how do you think God wants you to show love to each other? Why is it important to God that you show love to each other?

LIVING ON PURPOSE

Worship

Take time this week to embrace the truths that God is relational; he loves you; and he is your Father in heaven. Reflect on that and worship him in one of the following ways:

- In your personal prayers this week, try addressing God as Abba or even Daddy. (Don't think of it as irreverent; it's a word that expresses your intimate connection with and your ultimate dependence on God.)

- Some people find it helps to picture being in the presence of God. We don't worship the picture; it simply helps us to worship God. Picture God as your Father. Picture him walking up to you, taking your face tenderly in his hands, and asking you, "What do you want me to do for you today?"[2]

PRAYER DIRECTION

Take a few minutes to thank God for the blessings you enjoy as his child. If you have a new group, some members may not be used to praying out loud together yet. Begin this time of praise and thanks by just mentioning a few words or phrases like, "Thank you for loving me," or, "I praise you, Lord, for being a wonderful Father to me." Remember to keep your praises short so several others can participate.

---

[2] J. P. Moreland, Saddleback Church Men's Retreat, 7 February 2000.

NOTES

3

Session three

GOD IS A TRINITY

CATCHING UP

1. Did you find yourself thinking more about God as your Father this week? Share a place or circumstance in which you were reminded that he is your Father.

2. Were you able to share last week's truth about our relational God with someone else?

Key Verse

" . . . I am God, and there is no other;
I am God, and there is none like me."

Isaiah 46:9 (NIV)

GOD IS a TRINITY

BIBLE TEACHING
Watch the video lesson now and take notes in your outline on pages 23–27.

In the Bible, the most important story of all is _____ .

We looked in the last study at the clearest expression of the truth that God is personal: the fact that he is our Father. But there are other aspects of God's person that we all need to know and understand.

God Is a _____ .

A FRESH WORD
Trinity

God is three in one: the _____ , the _____ , and the _____ . He is not three Gods, nor is he one God acting in three different ways. The Bible tells us that God is three different and distinct persons, and that these three different and distinct persons are one in the being of God.

Pictures and Statements Regarding the Trinity

The doctrine of the Trinity is not found in any single verse of the Bible. It is instead found in a study of the whole of the Bible.

St. Patrick's picture of the Trinity was the three-leafed shamrock—three leaves tied together in one plant.

Some use the picture of the three forms of water: ice, liquid, and steam. Water under pressure and in a vacuum at a given temperature below freezing exists simultaneously as ice, liquid, and gas; yet it is identifiable always as water (H_2O), its basic nature. In physics this is called "the triple point of water."

Others use a much simpler picture: Neapolitan ice cream! The three flavors are distinct and separate, yet without any one of them it would not be Neapolitan.

> When I first began to study the Bible years ago, the doctrine of the Trinity was one of the most complex problems I had to encounter. I have never fully resolved it, for it contains an aspect of mystery. Though I do not totally understand it to this day, I accept it as a revelation of God.[3]
>
> — Billy Graham

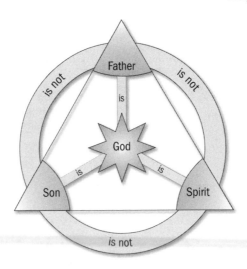

---

[3] Billy Graham, *The Holy Spirit: Activating God's Power in Your Life* (New York: Warner, 1980), 27–28.

The Truth of the Trinity Is Shown by the Bible's Teaching That . . .

1. God is _____ .

    . . . *The LORD our God, the LORD is one.* (Deuteronomy 6:4 NIV)

    "*. . . I am God, and there is no other; I am God, and there is none like me.*" (Isaiah 46:9 NIV)

2. The _____ , the _____ ,

    and the _____ are all called God.

    - The Father is God.

        . . . *Grace and peace to you from God our Father and from the Lord Jesus Christ.* (Romans 1:7 NIV)

    - Jesus is God.

        Thomas said to him, "My Lord and my God!" (John 20:28 NIV)

        In the beginning the Word already existed. He was with God, and he was God. (John 1:1 NLT)

    - The Spirit is God.

        [16]"*And I will ask the Father, and he will give you another Counselor to be with you forever—*[17]*the Spirit of truth. The world cannot accept him, because it neither sees him nor knows him. But you know him, for he lives with you and will be in you.*" (John 14:16–17 NIV)

        [3]*Then Peter said, "Ananias, how is it that Satan has so filled your heart that you have lied to the Holy Spirit . . .*[4]*You have not lied to men but to God.*" (Acts 5:3–4 NIV)

3. The Father, the Son, and the Holy Spirit are _____ from one another.

- Jesus is distinct from the Father. (He prayed to the Father in John 17.)

- The Spirit is distinct from the Father (John 14:26).

- The Son is distinct from the Spirit (John 14:16–17).

The conclusion is: God is one in being, but he exists in

_____ .

Glimpses of God at Work as a Trinity

- God speaks of himself as _____ in four places in the Old Testament (Genesis 1:26, 3:22, 11:7; Isaiah 6:8).

- All three persons were involved in Creation (the Spirit—Genesis 1:2; the Father—Hebrews 1:2; the Son—Colossians 1:15–16).

- We are _____ in the name of the Father, the Son, and the Spirit (Matthew 28:19).

- All three persons were at Jesus' _____ (Mark 1:10–11) and in Jesus' _____ (Luke 1:35).

- The Bible tells us all three persons were the power behind Jesus'

_____ . In John 2:19, Jesus said he would raise his body. In Romans 8:11 we're told that the Holy Spirit raised Jesus. In Acts 3:26, the Father raised the Son. This makes sense only when you understand the truth of the Trinity. Only God can raise someone from the dead.

- Paul's prayer in 2 Corinthians 13:14 (NIV): *May the grace of the Lord Jesus Christ, and the love of God, and the fellowship of the Holy Spirit be with you all.*

- Jesus' promise to his disciples in John 14:16–17: Jesus says he will ask the Father for the Spirit.

GOD IS a TRINITY

KEY PERSONAL PERSPECTIVE

Why Is This Important?
Reasons to Study the Trinity

Theologically: Understanding the truth of the Trinity prevents us from adopting

_____ of God.

It prevents us from seeing Jesus and the Spirit as less than God; from seeing Jesus and the Father as exactly the same; and from thinking that there are three Gods rather than just one.

One of our inevitable temptations as human beings is to see God as less than who he is. The truth of the Trinity helps us resist this temptation.

Personally: The Trinity is a reminder of the _____ and

_____ of the God who gave himself for us on the cross.

You trust the truth of the Trinity:

- When you ask for salvation (the Spirit convicts—John 16:8; the Son sacrifices—Hebrews 10:10; the Father gives—John 3:16).

- Every time you pray (the Spirit communicates—Romans 8:26; Jesus intercedes—Romans 8:34; the Father answers—John 16:23-24).

Relationally: The Trinity shows us that God in his very essence is

_____ .

Even before he created us, there was a perfect relationship between God the Father, God the Son, and God the Spirit. God did not need to create us in order to have someone to relate to, because he already had the perfect relationship in the Trinity. Our ability to relate to one another and to enjoy our relationship with God grows out of his relational nature.

DISCOVERY QUESTIONS

1. We have seen that God is one in being, but he exists in three persons. How does your understanding of each person of the Trinity give you confidence that God is able and willing to meet your needs? Where could expanded understanding help?

2. Understanding the Trinity is helpful when faced with questions about what you believe about God. Take a few minutes to think about how you would explain the Trinity to someone who might say to you, "Christians are polytheists: they believe in three gods." Write a brief answer below.

   (For a more in-depth look at the theology of the Trinity, refer to the appendix on page 44.)

3. Share one aspect of this week's study that was especially meaningful to you.

Did You Get It? How has this study helped you see why the truth of the Trinity is so important to our understanding of God? Can you recall any false teaching you may have heard about God that the truth of the Trinity helps to combat?

Share with Someone: Think of a person you can encourage with the truth you learned in this session. Write their name in the space below and pray for god to provide that opportunity this week.

LIVING ON PURPOSE

Discipleship

Read the *Key Verses* at the end of this study guide. Listen to what God might be speaking to your heart. Ask him for understanding and to show you what changes you can make to grow in your relationship with him. Record your thoughts or prayers in a journal.

PRAYER DIRECTION

Take a few minutes to focus on the person of God and his greatness. Share some things you are grateful for as you think about God as *real, revealed,* and *relational,* and how these characteristics are evident in the Trinity. In prayer, praise God for his characteristics and what they mean in your everyday life.

NOTES

Session four

4

CHARACTERISTICS OF GOD

CATCHING UP

1. Were you able to share last week's truth about the Trinity with someone else?

2. What did you learn from last week's "Living on Purpose" section?

Key Verse

You know when I sit and when I rise;
you perceive my thoughts from afar.
You discern my going out and my lying down;
you are familiar with all my ways.

Psalm 139:2–3 (NIV)

CHARACTERISTICS OF GOD

BIBLE TEACHING
Watch the video lesson now and take notes in your outline on pages 33–36.

God Is _____ .

Sovereignty refers not to God's attitude but to the reality of who he is. God is not someone with a dominating personality; he is a person who is absolutely dominant. God is not controlling; he is in ultimate control. God does not need to take charge because he is always in charge.

1. He is greater than and exists above his creation. He is

_____ .

> But will God really dwell on earth? The heavens, even the highest heaven, cannot contain you. How much less this temple I have built! (1 Kings 8:27 NIV)

> One God and Father of all, who is over all and through all and in all. (Ephesians 4:6 NIV)

- He is greater than time (Isaiah 57:15; Deuteronomy 33:27; Psalm 90:2).

- He is greater than place (Psalm 139:7–10; Jeremiah 23:23; Acts 17:24–28).

- He is greater than circumstance (James 1:17; 1 Samuel 15:29; Malachi 3:6).

Nothing _____ God.

> You know when I sit down and when I get up. You know my thoughts before I think them. (Psalm 139:2 NCV)

2. He never needs permission or help: he is _____ .

> *And he is not served by human hands, as if he needed anything, because he himself gives all men life and breath and everything else.* (Acts 17:25 NIV)

> *. . . Who are you, a mere human being, to criticize God? Should the thing that was created say to the one who made it, "Why have you made me like this?"* (Romans 9:20 NLT)

3. God can do anything he wants: he is _____ .

> *⁴He counts the stars and calls them all by name. ⁵How great is our Lord! His power is absolute! His understanding is beyond comprehension!* (Psalm 147:4–5 NLT)

A FRESH WORD

Words to Describe God

For just a moment, think again about the words we've been using to describe God. These words are often misunderstood. They have taken on meanings that make us feel that God is an impersonal God. This should be no surprise since one of Satan's schemes is to twist and degrade the name and person of God in order to lessen his impact in the world and in our lives. Here's the truth about some of the words we commonly use to describe God.

Holy does not mean God is picky or judgmental or "holier than thou." To be holy, literally, is to be separate and distinct. Holy means God has perfect integrity. In fact, he is the only being in the universe with perfect integrity.

Eternal does not mean that God is old or tired or out of date. God has always existed. He stands outside of time, able to see the entire history of the universe at a glance.

Transcendent does not mean that God cannot understand our needs and hurts. It does not mean, as in the Bette Midler song, that he's watching us "from a distance." The fact that God stands above and beyond his creation does not mean he stands outside his creation. He is both transcendent (above and beyond his creation) and immanent (within and throughout his creation).

Almighty does not mean that God does whatever he wants with no thought to the impact on us. He uses his power to create and to love his creation.

All-knowing does not mean that God is some kind of cosmic Big Brother, watching and judging us but never really caring about us. We know that as human beings we could not see all of the pain in the world without somehow becoming numb to it, but God is not like that. He can see all that happens and still deeply care about everything that happens.

God Is _____ .

"God is good, all the time.
All the time, God is good."

- He acts in _____ (Leviticus 11:44; Isaiah 6:1–3).

> [1]In the year that King Uzziah died, I saw the Lord seated on a
> throne, high and exalted, and the train of his robe filled the
> temple. [2]Above him were seraphs, each with six wings: With
> two wings they covered their faces, with two they covered their
> feet, and with two they were flying. [3]And they were calling to
> one another: "Holy, holy, holy is the LORD Almighty; the
> whole earth is full of his glory." (Isaiah 6:1–3 NIV)

- He relates in _____ (Exodus 34:6; Lamentations 3:22;
  James 5:11).

- His _____ can be trusted (Psalm 36:5;
  Hebrews 10:23).

- His _____ is unequaled (Psalm 34:8; 2 Peter 1:3).

- His _____ is impartial and fair (Isaiah 30:18;
  Luke 18:7–8).

- He reacts to sin in _____ (Genesis 6:5–8; Romans 2:5–9;
  1 Thessalonians 2:16).

- He is _____ (1 John 4:7–11; John 3:16).

DISCOVERY QUESTIONS

1. What concept from this session helped you better understand God's greatness?

2. What have you learned as we've studied together that will assist you in dealing with a specific situation you are facing right now? What have you learned that has increased your sense of security in everyday life?

3. When you were asked in the video to circle one of the qualities of God in which you would like to grow, which one did you circle? (See page 36.) How are you currently growing in love, holiness, compassion, and faithfulness? What can you do this week to further develop these qualities in your life?

4. As we come to the end of our look at the person of God, choose several of the following questions to answer and share as a group:

- What new thing did you learn about God?

- What did you learn that made God seem a little closer, a little less distant?

- What did you learn about God that made you able to enjoy him more?

- What did you learn about God that made you feel more loved by him?

- What did you learn about God that helped you understand his greatness more clearly?

- What did you learn about God that increased your desire to devote your life to him?

- What did you learn about God that increased your sense of security in everyday life?

5. Share one aspect of this week's study that was especially meaningful to you.

Did You Get It? How has this week's study helped you see the truths of God's sovereignty and goodness in new ways?

Share with Someone: Think of a person you can encourage with the truth you learned in this session. Write their name in the space below and pray for God to provide that opportunity this week.

LIVING ON PURPOSE

Evangelism

God desires for his character to be shown in the world. We have seen in this session that how God acts toward us is how he wants us to act toward others. Who do you know who needs to see God's character displayed to them (perhaps through compassion, love, goodness, or forgiveness) this week?

PRAYER DIRECTION

The prayers we pray that reflect God's character and his will for our lives are our most powerful prayers. Use the questions below to begin a prayer list for your group. It will be exciting for your group to see God begin to answer the prayers on this list.

- Where in this world (or in your world) would you most like to see people recognize God's compassion?

- Who do you most hope could connect with God's wisdom?

- Who or what are you counting on God to help you be patient with?

- What relationship would you most like to see God make right? (These could be relationships between individuals, groups, or even nations.)

- Who can you begin to pray for now?

NOTES

APPENDIX

APPENDIX

THEOLOGY OF THE TRINITY		
Introduction	The word *Trinity* is never used, nor is the doctrine of Trinitarianism ever explicitly taught, in the Scriptures, but Trinitarianism is the best explication [detailed explanation] of the biblical evidence. It is a crucial doctrine for Christianity because it focuses on who God is, and particularly on the deity of Jesus Christ. Because Trinitarianism is not taught explicitly in the Scriptures, the study of the doctrine is an exercise in putting together biblical themes and data through a systematic theological study and through looking at the historical development of the present orthodox view of what the biblical presentation of the Trinity is.	
Essential Elements of the Trinity	God is One. Each of the persons within the Godhead is Deity. The oneness of God and the threeness of God are not contradictory. The Trinity (Father, Son, and Holy Spirit) is eternal. Each of the persons of God is of the same essence and is not inferior or superior to the others in essence. The Trinity is a mystery which we will never be able to understand fully.	
Biblical Teaching	Old Testament	New Testament
God Is One	"Hear, O Israel: The LORD our God, the LORD is one." (Deuteronomy 6:4; cf. 20:2-4)	"Now to the King eternal, immortal, invisible, the only God, be honor and glory for ever and ever. Amen." (1 Timothy 1:17; cf. 1 Corinthians 8:4-6; 1 Timothy 2:5-6; James 2:19)

Biblical Teaching	Old Testament	New Testament
	The Father: "He said to me, 'You are my Son; today I have become your Father.'" (Psalm 2:7)	". . . who have been chosen according to the foreknowledge of God the Father." (1 Peter 1:2; cf. John 1:17–18; 1 Corinthians 8:6; Philippians 2:11)
Three Distinct Persons as Deity	**The Son:** "He said to me, 'You are my Son; today I have become your Father.'" (Psalm 2:7; cf. Hebrews 1:1–13; Psalm 68:18; Isaiah 6:1–3; 9:6)	"As soon as Jesus was baptized, he went up out of the water. At that moment heaven was opened, and he saw the Spirit of God descending like a dove and lighting on him. And a voice from heaven said, 'This is my Son, whom I love; with him I am well pleased.'" (Matthew 3:16–17)
	The Holy Spirit: "In the beginning God created the heavens and the earth . . . and the Spirit of God was hovering over the waters." (Genesis 1:1–2; cf. Exodus 31:3; Judges 15:14; Isaiah 11:2)	"Then Peter said, 'Ananias, how is it that Satan has so filled your heart that you have lied to the Holy Spirit . . . ? You have not lied to men but to God.'" (Acts 5:3–4; cf. 2 Corinthians 3:17)
Plurality of Persons in the Godhead	The use of plural pronouns points to, or at least suggests, the plurality of persons within the Godhead in the Old Testament. "Then God said, 'Let us make man in our image, in our likeness . . . ' " (Genesis 1:26)	The use of the singular word "name" when referring to God the Father, Son, and Holy Spirit indicates a unity within the threeness of God. "Therefore go and make disciples of all nations, baptizing them in the name of the Father and of the Son and of the Holy Spirit." (Matthew 28:19)

	Attribute	Father	Son	Holy Spirit
Persons of the Same Essence: Attributes Applied to Each Person	**Eternality**	Psalm 90:2	John 1:2; Revelation 1:8, 17	Hebrews 9:14
	Power	1 Peter 1:5	2 Corinthians 12:9	Romans 15:19
	Omniscience	Jeremiah 17:10	Revelation 2:23	1 Corinthians 2:11
	Omnipresence	Jeremiah 23:24	Matthew 18:20	Psalm 139:7
	Holiness	Revelation 15:4	Acts 3:14	Acts 1:8
	Truth	John 7:28	Revelation 3:7	1 John 5:6
	Benevolence	Romans 2:4	Ephesians 5:25	Nehemiah 9:20
Equality with Different Roles: Activities Involving	**Creation of Man**	Genesis 2:7	Colossians 1:16	Genesis 1:2; Job 26:13
	Creation of the World	Psalm 102:25	Colossians 1:16	Job 33:4
	Baptism of Christ	Matthew 3:17	Matthew 3:16–17	Matthew 3:16
	Death of Christ	Hebrews 9:14	Hebrews 9:14	Hebrews 9:14

Source: Taken from *Charts of Christian Theology and Doctrine* by H. Wayne House. Copyright © 1992 by H. Wayne House. Used by permission of Zondervan.

Small Group Resources

HELPS FOR HOSTS

Top Ten Ideas for New Hosts

Congratulations! As the host of your small group, you have responded to the call to help shepherd Jesus' flock. Few other tasks in the family of God surpass the contribution you will be making.

As you prepare to facilitate your group, whether it is one session or the entire series, here are a few thoughts to keep in mind. We encourage you to read and review these tips with each new discussion host before he or she leads.

Remember you are not alone. God knows everything about you, and he knew you would be asked to facilitate your group. Even though you may not feel ready, this is common for all good hosts. God promises, *"I will never leave you; I will never abandon you"* (Hebrews 13:5 TEV). Whether you are facilitating for one evening, several weeks, or a lifetime, you will be blessed as you serve.

1. **Don't try to do it alone.** Pray right now for God to help you build a healthy team. If you can enlist a cohost to help you shepherd the group, you will find your experience much richer. This is your chance to involve as many people as you can in building a healthy group. All you have to do is ask people to help. You'll be surprised at the response.

2. **Be friendly and be yourself.** God wants to use your unique gifts and temperament. Be sure to greet people at the door with a big smile . . . this can set the mood for the whole gathering. Remember, they are taking as big a step to show up at your house as you are to lead this group! Don't try to do things exactly like another host; do them in a way that fits you. Admit when you don't have an answer and apologize when you make a mistake. Your group will love you for it and you'll sleep better at night.

3. **Prepare for your meeting ahead of time.** Review the session and write down your responses to each question. Pay special attention to exercises that ask group members to do something other than engage in discussion. These exercises will help your group live what the Bible teaches, not just talk about it. Be sure you understand how an exercise works. If the exercise employs one of the items in the Small Group Resources section (such as the Group Guidelines), be sure to look over that item so you'll know how it works.

4. **Pray for your group members by name.** Before you begin your session, take a few moments and pray for each member by name. You may want to review the prayer list at least once a week. Ask God to use your time together to touch the heart of every person in your group. Expect God to lead you to whomever he wants you to encourage or challenge in a special way. If you listen, God will surely lead.

5. **When you ask a question, be patient.** Someone will eventually respond. Sometimes people need a moment or two of silence to think about the question. If silence doesn't bother you, it won't bother anyone else. After someone responds, affirm the response with a simple "thanks" or "great answer." Then ask, "How about somebody else?" or "Would someone who hasn't shared like to add anything?" Be sensitive to new people or reluctant members who aren't ready to say, pray, or do anything. If you give them a safe setting, they will blossom over time. If someone in your group is a "wallflower" who sits silently through every session, consider talking to them privately and encouraging them to participate. Let them know how important they are to you—that they are loved and appreciated—and that the group would value their input. Remember, still water often runs deep.

6. **Provide transitions between questions.** Ask if anyone would like to read the paragraph or Bible passage. Don't call on anyone, but ask for a volunteer, and then be patient until someone begins. Be sure to thank the person who reads aloud.

7. **Break into smaller groups occasionally.** With a greater opportunity to talk in a small circle, people will connect more with the study, apply more quickly what they're learning, and ultimately get more out of their small group experience. A small circle also encourages a quiet person to participate and tends to minimize the effects of a more vocal or dominant member.

8. **Small circles are also helpful during prayer time.** People who are unaccustomed to praying aloud will feel more comfortable trying it with just two or three others. Also, prayer requests won't take as much time, so circles will have more time to actually pray. When you gather back with the whole group, you can have one person from each circle briefly update everyone on the prayer requests from their subgroups. The other great aspect of subgrouping is that it fosters leadership development. As you ask people in the group to facilitate discussion or to lead a prayer circle, it gives them a small leadership step that can build their confidence.

9. **Rotate facilitators occasionally.** You may be perfectly capable of hosting each time, but you will help others grow in their faith and gifts if you give them opportunities to host the group.

10. **One final challenge (for new or first-time hosts).** Before your first opportunity to lead, look up each of the six passages that follow. Read each one as a devotional exercise to help prepare you with a shepherd's heart. Trust us on this one. If you do this, you will be more than ready for your first meeting.

Matthew 9:36–38 (NIV)
[36]When Jesus saw the crowds, he had compassion on them, because they were harassed and helpless, like sheep without a shepherd. [37]Then he said to his disciples, "The harvest is plentiful but the workers are few. [38]Ask the Lord of the harvest, therefore, to send out workers into his harvest field."

John 10:14–15 (NIV)
[14]I am the good shepherd; I know my sheep and my sheep know me—[15]just as the Father knows me and I know the Father—and I lay down my life for the sheep.

1 Peter 5:2–4 (NIV)

²Be shepherds of God's flock that is under your care, serving as overseers—not because you must, but because you are willing, as God wants you to be; ³not greedy for money, but eager to serve; not lording it over those entrusted to you, but being examples to the flock. ⁴And when the Chief Shepherd appears, you will receive the crown of glory that will never fade away.

Philippians 2:1–5 (NIV)

¹If you have any encouragement from being united with Christ, if any comfort from his love, if any fellowship with the Spirit, if any tenderness and compassion, ²then make my joy complete by being like-minded, having the same love, being one in spirit and purpose. ³Do nothing out of selfish ambition or vain conceit, but in humility consider others better than yourselves. ⁴Each of you should look not only to your own interests, but also to the interests of others. ⁵Your attitude should be the same as that of Jesus Christ.

Hebrews 10:23–25 (NIV)

²³Let us hold unswervingly to the hope we profess, for he who promised is faithful. ²⁴And let us consider how we may spur one another on toward love and good deeds. ²⁵Let us not give up meeting together, as some are in the habit of doing, but let us encourage one another—and all the more as you see the Day approaching.

1 Thessalonians 2:7–8, 11–12 (NIV)

⁷. . . but we were gentle among you, like a mother caring for her little children. ⁸We loved you so much that we were delighted to share with you not only the gospel of God but our lives as well, because you had become so dear to us. . . . ¹¹For you know that we dealt with each of you as a father deals with his own children, ¹²encouraging, comforting and urging you to live lives worthy of God, who calls you into his kingdom and glory.

FREQUENTLY ASKED QUESTIONS

How long will this group meet?

This volume of *Foundations: God* is four sessions long. We encourage your group to add a fifth session for a celebration. In your final session, each group member may decide if he or she desires to continue on for another study. At that time you may also want to do some informal evaluation, discuss your Group Guidelines, and decide which study you want to do next. We recommend you visit our website at **www.saddlebackresources.com** for more video-based small group studies.

Who is the host?

The host is the person who coordinates and facilitates your group meetings. In addition to a host, we encourage you to select one or more group members to lead your group discussions. Several other responsibilities can be rotated, including refreshments, prayer requests, worship, or keeping up with those who miss a meeting. Shared ownership in the group helps everybody grow.

Where do we find new group members?

Recruiting new members can be a challenge for groups, especially new groups with just a few people, or existing groups that lose a few people along the way. We encourage you to use the *Circles of Life* diagram on page 56 of this DVD study guide to brainstorm a list of people from your workplace, church, school, neighborhood, family, and so on. Then pray for the people on each member's list. Allow each member to invite several people from their list. Some groups fear that newcomers will interrupt the intimacy that members have built over time. However, groups that welcome newcomers generally gain strength with the infusion of new blood. Remember, the next person you add just might become a friend for eternity. Logistically, groups find different ways to add members. Some groups remain permanently open, while others choose to open periodically, such as at the beginning or end of a study. If your group becomes too large for easy, face-to-face conversations, you can subgroup, forming a second discussion group in another room.

How do we handle the child care needs in our group?

Child care needs must be handled very carefully. This is a sensitive issue. We suggest you seek creative solutions as a group. One common solution is to have the adults meet in the living room and share the cost of a babysitter (or two) who can be with the kids in another part of the house. Another popular option is to have one home for the kids and a second home (close by) for the adults. If desired, the adults could rotate the responsibility of providing a lesson for the kids. This last option is great with school-age kids and can be a huge blessing to families.

GROUP GUIDELINES

It's a good idea for every group to put words to their shared values, expectations, and commitments. Such guidelines will help you avoid unspoken agendas and unmet expectations. We recommend you discuss your guidelines during Session One in order to lay the foundation for a healthy group experience. Feel free to modify anything that does not work for your group.

We agree to the following values:

Clear Purpose To grow healthy spiritual lives by building a healthy small group community

Group Attendance To give priority to the group meeting (call if I am absent or late)

Safe Environment To create a safe place where people can be heard and feel loved (no quick answers, snap judgments, or simple fixes)

Be Confidential To keep anything that is shared strictly confidential and within the group

Conflict Resolution To avoid gossip and to immediately resolve any concerns by following the principles of Matthew 18:15–17

Spiritual Health To give group members permission to speak into my life and help me live a healthy, balanced spiritual life that is pleasing to God

Limit Our Freedom To limit our freedom by not serving or consuming alcohol during small group meetings or events so as to avoid causing a weaker brother or sister to stumble (1 Corinthians 8:1–13; Romans 14:19–21)

Welcome Newcomers   To invite friends who might benefit from this study and warmly welcome newcomers

Building Relationships To get to know the other members of the group and pray for them regularly

Other   _____

We have also discussed and agreed on the following items:

Child Care

_____

_____

Starting Time

_____

Ending Time

_____

If you haven't already done so, take a few minutes to fill out the *Small Group Calendar* on page 60.

CIRCLES OF LIFE—SMALL GROUP CONNECTIONS

Discover who you can connect in community

Use this chart to help carry out one of the values in the Group Guidelines to "Welcome Newcomers."

"Follow me, and I will make you fishers of men." (Matthew 4:19 KJV)

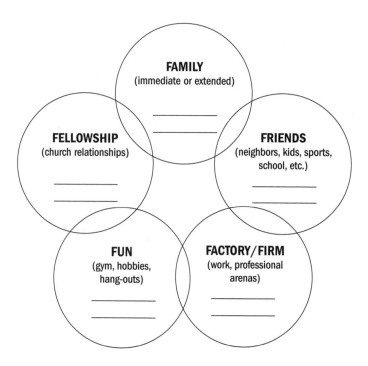

Follow this simple three-step process:

1. List 1–2 people in each circle.

2. Prayerfully select one person or couple from your list and tell your group about them.

3. Give them a call and invite them to your next meeting. Over 50 percent of those invited to a small group say, "Yes!"

SMALL GROUP PRAYER AND PRAISE REPORT

This is a place where you can write each other's requests for prayer. You can also make a note when God answers a prayer. Pray for each other's requests. If you're new to group prayer, it's okay to pray silently or to pray by using just one sentence: "God, please help

_____ to _____."

DATE	PERSON	PRAYER REQUEST	PRAISE REPORT

foundations GOD

SMALL GROUP PRAYER AND PRAISE REPORT

DATE	PERSON	PRAYER REQUEST	PRAISE REPORT

SMALL GROUP PRAYER AND PRAISE REPORT

DATE	PERSON	PRAYER REQUEST	PRAISE REPORT

SMALL GROUP CALENDAR

Healthy groups share responsibilities and group ownership. It might take some time for this to develop. Shared ownership ensures that responsibility for the group doesn't fall to one person. Use the calendar to keep track of social events, mission projects, birthdays, or days off. Complete this calendar at your first or second meeting. Planning ahead will increase attendance and shared ownership.

DATE	LESSON	LOCATION	FACILITATOR	SNACK OR MEAL
5/4	Session 2	Chris and Andrea	Jim Brown	Phil and Karen

ANSWER KEY

Session One: What Is God Like?

Children have a way of asking all the <u>right questions</u>.

1. God is <u>real</u>.
2. God is <u>revealed</u>.
3. God is <u>relational</u>.

1. We see God's <u>creativity</u> in what he has made.
2. We see God's <u>thumbprint</u> on human history.
3. We've seen God's <u>actions</u> in our own lives.

1. God's <u>general revelation</u> of himself.
2. God reveals himself through <u>his Word</u>.
3. God reveals himself through <u>his Son</u>.

Session Two: God Is Relational

3. God is <u>RELATIONAL</u>.

The truth is: God is <u>near</u>.

The truth is: God is intimately involved in <u>every detail</u> of our lives.

The truth is: God is waiting to <u>forgive</u> all who ask.

The truth is: God allows . . . more people might be <u>saved</u> out of it.

God's <u>Immanence</u>: God is awesomely near to all of us.

God's <u>Omnipresence</u>: God is everywhere.

God's <u>Omniscience</u>: God knows everything.

God's <u>Omnipotence</u>: God is almighty.

- In a world in which people see God as <u>unapproachable</u>, the truth is that God is <u>relational</u>.
- Jesus taught us to call God our <u>Father</u>.

1. Our Father is willing to make <u>sacrifices</u>.
2. Our Father has <u>compassion</u> and <u>love</u> for his children.
3. Our Father <u>guides</u> his children.
4. Our Father knows <u>our needs</u> before we ask.
5. Our Father <u>rewards</u> us.
6. Our Father makes us <u>his heirs</u>.
7. Our Father <u>encourages</u> us.
8. Our Father shows no <u>favoritism</u> among his children.

Worship is <u>acting</u> like God is your Father.

Session Three: God Is a Trinity

In the Bible, the most important story of all is <u>God's story</u>.

God Is a <u>Trinity</u>

God is three in one: the <u>Father</u>, the <u>Son</u>, and the <u>Holy Spirit</u>.

1. God is <u>one</u>.
2. The <u>Father</u>, the <u>Son</u>, and the <u>Spirit</u> are all called God.
3. The Father, the Son, and the Holy Spirit are <u>distinct</u> from one another.

God is one in being, but he exists in <u>three persons</u>.

- God speaks of himself as <u>us</u> in four places in the Old Testament.
- We are <u>baptized</u> in the name of the Father, the Son, and the Spirit.
- All three persons were at Jesus' <u>baptism</u> and in Jesus' <u>birth announcement</u>.
- The Bible tells us all three persons were the power behind Jesus' <u>resurrection</u>.

Understanding the truth of the Trinity prevents us from adopting <u>inadequate views</u> of God.

The Trinity is a reminder of the <u>majesty</u> and <u>mystery</u> of the God who gave himself for us on the cross.

The Trinity shows us that God in his very essence is <u>relational</u>.

Session 4: Characteristics of God

God Is <u>Absolutely Sovereign</u>.

1. He is greater than and exists above his creation. He is <u>transcendent</u>.

   Nothing <u>surprises</u> God.

2. He never needs permission or help: he is <u>all-sufficient</u>.

3. God can do anything he wants: he is <u>almighty</u>.

God Is <u>Perfectly Moral</u>.

- He acts in <u>holiness</u>.
- He relates in <u>compassion</u>.
- His <u>faithfulness</u> can be trusted.
- His <u>goodness</u> is unequaled.
- His <u>justice</u> is impartial and fair.
- He reacts to sin in <u>wrath</u>.
- He is <u>love</u>.

NOTES

KEY VERSES

One of the most effective ways to drive deeply into our lives the principles we are learning in this series is to memorize key Scriptures. For many, memorization is a new concept or one that has been difficult in the past. We encourage you to stretch yourself and try to memorize these four key verses. If possible, memorize these as a group and make them part of your group time. You may cut these apart and carry them in your wallet.

I have hidden your word in my heart that I might not sin against you.

Psalm 119:11 (NIV)

Session One

The heavens declare the glory of God; the skies proclaim the work of his hands.

Psalm 19:1 (NIV)

Session Two

How great is the love the Father has lavished on us, that we should be called children of God! And that is what we are! The reason the world does not know us is that it did not know him.

1 John 3:1 (NIV)

Session Three

". . . I am God, and there is no other; I am God, and there is none like me."

Isaiah 46:9 (NIV)

Session Four

You know when I sit and when I rise; you perceive my thoughts from afar. You discern my going out and my lying down; you are familiar with all my ways.

Psalm 139:2–3 (NIV)

NOTES

We value your thoughts about what you've just read.
Please email us at *zauthor@zondervan.com*.

The Purpose Driven® Life
A six-session video-based study for groups or individuals

Embark on a journey of discovery with this video-based study taught by Rick Warren. In it you will discover the answer to life's most fundamental question: "What on earth am I here for?"

And here's a clue to the answer: It's not about you . . . You were created by God and for God, and until you understand that, life will never make sense. It is only in God that we discover our origin, our identity, our meaning, our purpose, our significance, and our destiny."

Whether you experience this adventure with a small group or on your own, this six-session, video-based study will change your life.

DVD Study Guide: 978-0-310-27866-5
DVD: 978-0-310-27864-1

Be sure to combine this study with your reading of the best-selling book, *The Purpose Driven® Life*, to give you or your small group the opportunity to discuss the implications and applications of living the life God created you to live.

Hardcover, Jacketed: 978-0-310-20571-5
Softcover: 978-0-310-27699-9

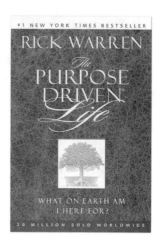

Pick up a copy today at your favorite bookstore!

ZONDERVAN®
.com

Foundations: 11 Core Truths to Build Your Life On

Taught by Tom Holladay and Kay Warren

Foundations is a series of 11 four-week video studies covering the most important, foundational doctrines of the Christian faith. Study topics include:

The Bible—This study focuses on where the Bible came from, why it can be trusted, and how it can change your life.
DVD Study Guide: 978-0-310-27670-8
DVD: 978-0-310-27669-2

God—This study focuses not just on facts about God, but on how to know God himself in a more powerful and personal way.
DVD Study Guide: 978-0-310-27672-2
DVD: 978-0-310-27671-5

Jesus—As we look at what the Bible says about the person of Christ, we do so as people who are developing a lifelong relationship with Jesus.
DVD Study Guide: 978-0-310-27674-6
DVD: 978-0-310-27673-9

The Holy Spirit—This study focuses on the person, the presence, and the power of the Holy Spirit, and how you can be filled with the Holy Spirit on a daily basis.
DVD Study Guide: 978-0-310-27676-0
DVD: 978-0-310-27675-3

Creation—Each of us was personally created by a loving God. This study does not shy away from the great scientific and theological arguments that surround the creation/evolution debate. However, you will find the goal of this study is deepening your awareness of God as your Creator.
DVD Study Guide: 978-0-310-27678-4
DVD: 978-0-310-27677-7

Pick up a copy today at your favorite bookstore!

Salvation—This study focuses on God's solution to man's need for salvation, what Jesus Christ did for us on the cross, and the assurance and security of God's love and provision for eternity.

DVD Study Guide: 978-0-310-27682-1
DVD: 978-0-310-27679-1

Sanctification—This study focuses on the two natures of the Christian. We'll see the difference between grace and law, and how these two things work in our lives.

DVD Study Guide: 978-0-310-27684-5
DVD: 978-0-310-27683-8

Good and Evil—Why do bad things happen to good people? Through this study we'll see how and why God continues to allow evil to exist. The ultimate goal is to build up our faith and relationship with God as we wrestle with these difficult questions.

DVD Study Guide: 978-0-310-27687-6
DVD: 978-0-310-27686-9

The Afterlife—The Bible does not answer all the questions we have about what happens to us after we die; however, this study deals with what the Bible does tell us. This important study gives us hope and helps us move from a focus on the here and now to a focus on eternity.

DVD Study Guide: 978-0-310-27689-0
DVD: 978-0-310-27688-3

The Church—This study focuses on the birth of the church, the nature of the church, and the mission of the church.

DVD Study Guide: 978-0-310-27692-0
DVD: 978-0-310-27691-3

The Second Coming—This study addresses both the hope and the uncertainties surrounding the second coming of Jesus Christ.

DVD Study Guide: 978-0-310-27695-1
DVD: 978-0-310-27693-7

Pick up a copy today at your favorite bookstore!

ZONDERVAN®
.com

Celebrate Recovery, Updated Curriculum Kit

This kit will provide your church with the tools necessary to start a successful Celebrate Recovery program. *Kit includes:*

- Introductory Guide for Leaders DVD
- Leader's Guide
- 4 Participant's Guides (one of each guide)
- CD-ROM with 25 lessons
- CD-ROM with sermon transcripts
- 4-volume audio CD sermon series

Curriculum Kit: 978-0-310-26847-5

Participant's Guide 4-pack

The Celebrate Recovery Participant's Guide 4-pack is a convenient resource when you're just getting started or if you need replacement guides for your program.

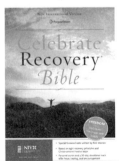

Celebrate Recovery Bible

With features based on eight principles Jesus voiced in his Sermon on the Mount, the new Celebrate Recovery bible offers hope, encouragement, and empowerment for those struggling with the circumstances of their livesand the habits they are trying to control.

Hardcover: 978-0-310-92849-2
Softcover: 978-0-310-93810-1

Pick up a copy today at your favorite bookstore!

Stepping Out of Denial into God's Grace

Participant's Guide 1 introduces the eight principles of recovery based on Jesus' words in the Beatitudes, and focuses on principles 1–3. Participants learn about denial, hope, sanity, and more.

Getting Right with God, Yourself, and Others

Participant's Guide 3 covers principles 5–7 based on Jesus' words in the Beatitudes. With courage and support from their fellow participants, people seeking recovery will find victory, forgiveness, and grace.

Taking an Honest and Spiritual Inventory

Participant's Guide 2 focuses on the fourth principle based on Jesus' words in the Beatitudes and builds on the Scripture, *"Happy are the pure in heart."* (Matthew 5:8) The participant will learn an invaluable principle for recovery and also take an in-depth spiritual inventory.

Growing in Christ While Helping Others

Participant's Guide 4 walks through the final steps of the eight recovery principles based on Jesus' words in the Beatitudes. In this final phase, participants learn to move forward in newfound freedom in Christ, learning how to give back to others. There's even a practical lesson called "Seven reasons we get stuck in our recoveries."

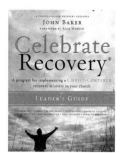

Leader's Guide

The Celebrate Recovery Leader's Guide gives you everything you need to facilitate your preparation time. Virtually walking you through every meeting, the Leader's Guide is a must-have for every leader on your Celebrate Recovery ministry team.

Pick up a copy today at your favorite bookstore!

Wide Angle:
Framing Your Worldview

Christianity is much more than a religion. It is a worldview—a way of seeing all of life and the world around you. Your worldview impacts virtually every decision you make in life: moral decisions, relational decisions, financial decisions— everything. How you see the world determines how you face the world.

In this brand new study, Rick Warren and Chuck Colson discuss such key issues as moral relativism, tolerance, terrorism, creationism vs. Darwinism, sin and suffering. They explore in depth the Christian worldview as it relates to the most important questions in life:

- Why does it matter what I believe?
- How do I know what's true?
- Where do I come from?
- Why is the world so messed up?
- Is there a solution?
- What is my purpose in life?

This study is as deep as it is wide, addressing vitally important topics for every follower of Christ.

Rick Warren   *Chuck Colson*

DVD Study Guide: 978-1-4228-0083-6
DVD: 978-1-4228-0082-9